I.T. RISKS LOGICAL ANALY

ISBN: 978-1-4717-1957-8

Copyright   ©   Andreas Sofroniou 2012

All rights reserved.

Making unauthorised copies is prohibited. No parts of this publication may be reproduced, transmitted, transcribed, stored in a retrieval system, translated in any language, or computer language, in any form, or by any means, without the prior written permission of

Andreas Sofroniou.

Copyright   ©   Andreas Sofroniou 2012

I.T. RISKS LOGICAL ANALYSIS

ISBN: 978-1-4717-1957-8

CONTENTS: **PAGE:**

1 RISKS LOGICAL ANALYSIS

1.1 PROGRAMME MANAGEMENT

Programme Management may have many responsibilities, but the most important of all is the ability to identify and positively execute plans to manage the risks threatening the objectives.

Through a process of structured interviews and plans the Assessment Analysis is used to highlight the specific Events which may turn into Risks. During the interviews Assessment Analysis is used to capture the key Events from the interviewees.

In turn, the Assessment Analysis provides a life-cycle process, which highlights the primary prioritisation of the risks. In large, complex, and critical programmes, it is essential that a true prioritised report is available so that the imminent threats can be managed first.

The process commences by identifying the most important events which may become threats to a project. These are given priority, support and management expertise. Once the prioritisation exercise is completed, the participating people are notified and subsequently interviewed to bring out and capture any possible concerns they may have.

Within a programme, projects are prioritised to ensure that those most critical to the programme's success are given priority to scarce resources.

1.2 RISK MANAGEMENT METHODOLOGY

The I.T. Risks Logical Analysis allows the capture of collective knowledge and expertise from those involved on the project, in a form that facilitates the communication of Events, Assessments and the pro-active management of risks. This method can be applied to any type of project, or programme.

In essence, this is the mechanism by which the functions of programmes and projects are held together as a result of the principles operating within the I.T. risk analysis methodology.

This is the systematic approach to the varied Events, their Assessments, and the consequential risks relating to or consisting of a system. Methodical in procedures and plans, these are addressed to those involved and deliberating within the parameters of their systems development responsibilities.

The results being dependable on the interaction and the mutual or reciprocal action which encourages those involved in the programmes and projects to communicate with each other and to work closely with a view to solving the threatening Events before they impact on the development of the system.

The individuals involved maintain a generic approach, which relates and characterises the whole group of those involved in assessing the Events and attacking the threatening ones before they become Risks to the development of the system. The end result being the avoidance of apparent problems within the pre-defined users' systems requirements.

This is enabled by following the I.T. Risk Management methodology. The system architects and the risk management practitioners simply follow the approved body of systems development methods, rules and management procedures employed by their organisation. For practical or even ethical reasons, it must be noted that with such a philosophy, it is seldom possible to fulfil all requirements of very large organisational systems.

As such, the I.T. Risk Management methodology is administered in applications; putting to use such techniques and in applying the Risk Management principles in the development of various applications will involve numerous and varied activities. A concrete issue in developing new applications is the problem of communication among the people involved, the motivation constantly needed for *generic* work, the ability to *interact systematically* and in using a structured systems *methodology*.

1.3 RISK MANAGEMENT CYCLE

The concept being a simple one as shown in the diagram below:

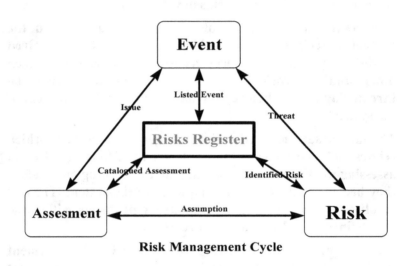

Risk Management Cycle

The I.T. Risk Management methodology was developed by the author whilst employed by *PsySys Limited,* over a period of some thirty years. The methodology was used for PsySys' international clients, from 1982 onwards. The idea of a structured approached to organisational problems proved beneficial to customers and users who integrated the full process with other methodologies, such as Structured Systems Analysis and Designing methods and Project Management procedures.

1.4 INTEGRATION OF METHODOLOGIES

The comprehension of how to integrate the three methodologies can be achieved, simply by following the concept as shown on the following diagrammatic representation:

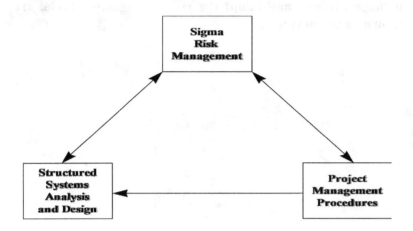

Integration Of Methodologies

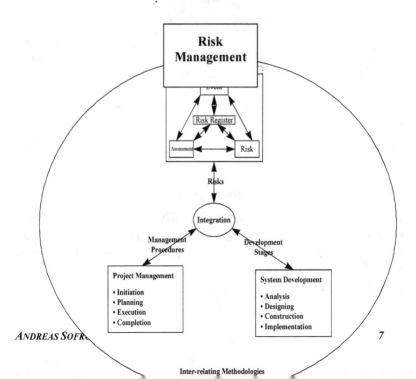

Inter-relating Methodologies

1.5 INTER-RELATIONSHIP

The various steps included in each of the methodologies are named in the next diagram. Or, to a further extent, the various stages of system development and the steps taken to manage projects and adopt the risk management cycle, are shown on the next page:

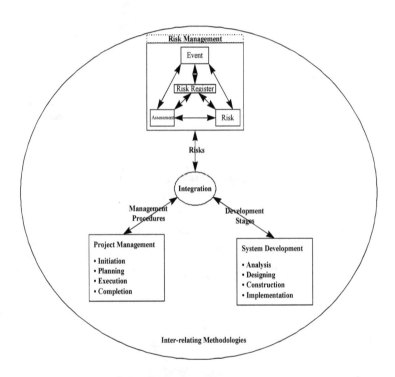

1.6 MANAGING THE RISK PROGRAMME

It is basic business sense to identify, assess, manage, and monitor risks that are significant to the fulfilment of an organisation's business objectives. In recent years businesses have been transformed by, and are in many cases heavily dependent on I.T.

The financial consequences of a breakdown in controls or a security breach are not only the loss incurred, but also the costs of recovering and preventing further failures. The impact is not only financial: it can affect adversely reputation and brand value as well as the business' performance and future potential.

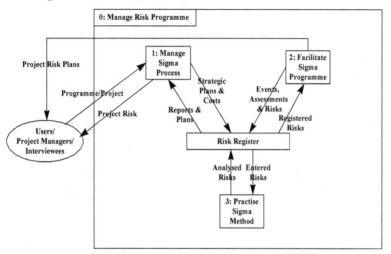

(The term *'Sigma'* used in the process boxes in some diagrams is based on the *PsySys* method of Risk Management.)

1.7 IMPACT ON BUSINESS

Organisations can regard inadequate system development as a significant risk, and where directors feel that this may be the situation in their businesses, they may need to ask tough questions of themselves and their management teams. Systems development and their risks is an issue that companies may need to recognise should regularly be on their agenda, and not delegated to I.T. technicians.

Business in the past was primarily confined to assessment of the risk surrounding fire, flood, and Acts of God. In business today we have become dependent on information systems. Failure to build computer systems as required by the users has a major impact on our business to function. The inability of companies to provide adequate systems can cause potential problems to customers, suppliers, employees and an all round havoc to information.

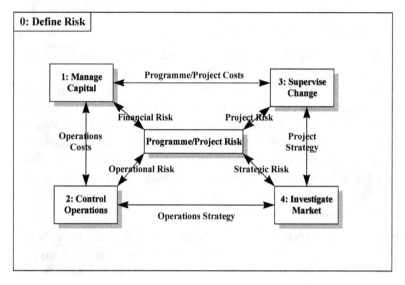

Programme/Project Risk: One Component Of The Total Business Risk.

2 RISK ANALYSES

2.1 ASSESSMENT OF RISKS

Fundamental to the creation of a Risk Management system is the assessment of the risks (Risks Analysis) to your business and the potential loss that could accrue if things go wring. Risk Assessment software tools are available in the market, which can be used by consultants, or by internal staff. What is important is the ability to assess the risk to your business and the cost to protect it against the risk. The end result is that you have to make the valued judgement on the amount the business spends on the implementation and the monitoring of a risk policy.

Products and systems are available to counter the threats and risks that have been identified. There is a wide range of options available, but remember that anything chosen will require expertise to design and complete a system, taking into account how the various solutions will inter-react with each other. Like all things to do with I.T., the design and implementation of systems' risk solutions is only as good as the people installing them.

2.2 COMMUNICATION

The MOST important factor in the success of any management style is the ability to communicate with each other, one to one or in groups of people. The art of communication is just as important to the whole process of the management of risks. More so where the risks identified have become a threat because of the problem of human communications.

This is where the appointment of an experienced and trained Risk Practitioner is worth the effort put into securing such individual/s.

2.3 RISKS MANAGEMENT PRACTICE

A trained Practitioner will have enough knowledge to run and maintain the system, as well as ample experience to be able to communicate with all levels of employees, hold meetings, and ensure the plans executed.

In brief and as the diagram on the next page shows, the Practitioner will be responsible for the complete Risk Management cycle.

2.4 RISK MANAGEMENT CYCLE

In analysing risks, certain counter measures may have to be looked into. The mechanisms for safeguarding the construction of your information system are by managing risks and avoiding the threat of failing to build the required system.

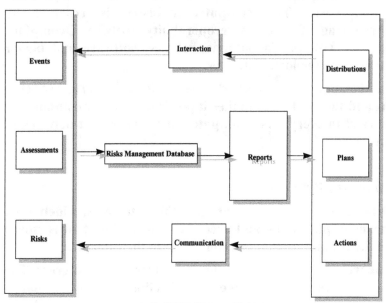

The Full Risk Management Cycle

2.5 INTERNET COMMERCE

Internet Commerce is a key component of the Global Networked Business model, providing a company's customers and partners with end-to-end solutions to conduct business transactions and exchange of information.

As a background, probably the main driver for building the Internet Global Commerce model has been the need for continuous business improvement, leading to cost savings achieved by changes in the supply chain.

Global businesses and manufacturing techniques now ensure that the business works twenty-four hours, by seven days, by fifty-two weeks basis, which can only be effectively managed by the integration of computer systems on the equivalent global basis. The computer industry is reacting by introducing further interoperability between computer systems with the introduction of new software and bigger capacity technological devices.

Further on, the Internet, this network of networks stretches around the world and makes it possible for every computer to connect to every other computer. It is the biggest network in the world.

2.6 WORLD WIDE WEB

Often confused with the Internet, this is the most widely used means of publishing and accessing information that is stored on the computers that are connected to the Internet.

The web allows you to link to many sites on the Internet. The basic concept is the page or collection of screens that it displays on your monitor. Within each page are links to related pages and other web sites. Each of these links is known as a hypertext link.

The web was originally used for text links only, but as it was further developed multimedia links were added. The web now contains pictures, audio and video links. With the addition of sound and graphics the web soon became the most popular way of linking to resources on the Internet.

Most organisations are worried by threats presented in using the web. Viruses are one of the main concerns, although these are unlikely to occur in normal surfing, except perhaps where Word and Excel documents are downloaded. Unauthorised access by outsiders is another.

Many organisations are also concerned about the employees wasting time surfing inappropriate web sites. To overcome this problem some companies choose to install a Content Security product that checks for ratings, profanity, and legal disclaimers.

2.7 BUSINESS CASE

The business case for justifying the expenditure on implementing a Risk Management system and the practising procedures to go with it in the early days of system development was more a leap of faith than a carefully evaluated financial case, and in many cases this may still be so.

Consultancy assignments and studies show that only a small percentage of organisations world-wide are taking this subject seriously. It is hoped that the information in this book will encourage you to review the Risk Management policy within your company.

2.8 GLOBAL NETWORKED BUSINESS

A Global Networked Business is a company, of any size, whose networked infrastructure and use of technology speeds up the process of communication, and the sharing of knowledge-between prospects, customers, employees, partners and suppliers.

A Global Networked Business uses networks and information technology to:

• Empower people to use and share information and to act more decisively,

• Transcend traditional barriers – including geographic, financial or organisational barriers,

• Increase responsiveness to customer needs and business opportunities,

• Compete more effectively in the global marketplace,

• Enables its customers, partners, employees, and suppliers to access information, resources and services in ways that work best for them.

2.9 IMPLEMENTATION OF RISK STRATEGY

The success, or failure, surrounding a Risk Management Strategy depends almost entirely on people, those who are designing and developing it and those who are expected to implement it. If the system is designed in such a way as to be too complicated to understand and comply with, or in such a way that makes it almost impossible to do ones job, then it will be rejected by those who should implement it.

Implementation of the policy is likely to involve modification of employment contracts. Monitoring the passage of information in and out of the organisation will involve human communication as well as technological means of communicating, such as the analysis of e-mails sent by employees, which can infringe their human rights, as can monitoring which sites are accessed on the Internet.

Care in selecting those who implement the Risk Management principles can substantially influence the level of confidence attained. The programmes require parameters to be set and therefore the level of understanding of your business requirements and the software will influence policies success or otherwise.

The communication exercise to the employees is probably the most important part of the implementation. If left to the I.T. department, it may be delivered in seem-technical language or in terms of the needs of the business, rather than in terms and language to which employees can relate. Failure to allocate sufficient budgets to this area can put the success of a risk management policy in jeopardy. It is also important to remember to include training in this area as part of the employees' induction.

Adoption of a Code of Ethics can be a useful adjunct to the process, as can the use of an external communication company.

3. METHODOLOGY EXPLAINED

3.1 PROGRAMME OBJECTIVES

It is a fact that most large, complex projects and programs fail to meet their planned objectives and as a consequence, most organisations are undertaking one or more aggressive programs at any point in time. These may fundamentally change the way the company conducts its business and failure to meet objectives on time may lead to a catastrophic loss of business.

Some projects or programmes can be chaotic at times. Objectives are evolving and plans and priorities are constantly changing. There is a temptation to accept this chaos as a necessary 'nature of the beast'. However, it is essential to move the programme forward in a traditional project management way by making sure that objectives and plans move forward.

Once we have clear objectives and plans, programme managers must control two fundamental factors if they are to be successful:

- The business plan must be clearly identified,

- The implementation of the program must be made explicit.

This can be answered by isolating the fundamental cause of most, if not all major project problems. It can be argued that projects only fail due to two fundamental reasons:

- The plans are proven to be incorrect,

- The significance of these plans is misunderstood.

The capture, analysis, and communication of such assessments are, therefore, critical to the success of any project. This forms the basis of the Risk Management methodology. The Risk method has been applied by PsySys to help many diverse organisations to deliver large, complex projects and programmes on time, to budget and in meeting the expectations of demanding users.

3.2 METHODOLOGY

The focus of the methodology is based on he capture and analysis of the critical events and their assessments within the project plans, processes, and procedures.

The methodology is essentially a framework process that allows the capture of collective knowledge and viewpoints from those involved on the project, in a form that facilitates communication of events, assessments and ensures the pro-active management of risks. This is accomplished by dramatically improving communications, risks are avoided or managed to the optimum, and project objectives are delivered on time.

In essence, this is the mechanism by which the functions of programmes and projects are held together as a result of the principles operating within the *I.T. Risk Management* methodology:

The varied events, their assessments, and the consequential risks relating to or consisting of a system. Methodical in procedures and plans, these are addressed to those involved and deliberating within the parameters of their systems development responsibilities.

The results being dependable on interaction. The mutual or reciprocal action which encourages those involved in the programmes and projects to communicate with each other and to work closely with a view to solving the threatening events before they impact on the development of the system.

The individuals involved maintain a generic approach, which relates and characterises the whole group of those involved in assessing the events and attacking the threatening ones before they become risks to the development of the system. The end result being the avoidance of apparent problems within the pre-defined users' systems requirements.

This is enabled by following the methodology. The system architects and the risk management practitioners simply follow the approved body of systems development methods, rules and management procedures employed by their organisation. For practical or even ethical reasons, it must be noted that with such a philosophy, it is seldom possible to fulfil all requirements of very large organisational systems.

As such, the risk methodology is administered in applications. Putting to use such techniques and in applying the risk management principles in the development of various *applications* will involve numerous and varied activities. A concrete issue in developing new applications is the problem of communication among the people involved, the motivation constantly needed for *generic* work, the ability to *interact systematically* and in using a structured systems *methodology.*

3.3 RISK MANAGEMENT CYCLE

Risk Management Cycle

3.4 FEATURES AND BENEFITS APPROACH

The key features and benefits of the PsySys approach are:

☐ *Communication* — Provides a simple, common, language for the communication of risk up, down and sideways within the organisation, whilst avoiding the normal problems of political sensitivity and risk aversion.

☐ *Control* — Enhances project control by exception management and achieves an overview of risk at senior management levels.

☐ *Information* — Encourages the sharing of risk information, establishing common objectives, discouraging risk transfer and hence reducing the overall risk to all involved parties.

☐ *Flexible* — An adaptable process which is rigorously applied to ensure that all significant risks are identified and controlled at the appropriate time.

☐ *Acceptable* — The non-intrusive/non-bureaucratic management process improves management discipline across the organization and is readily accepted by project teams.

3.5 ASSESSMENT ANALYSIS

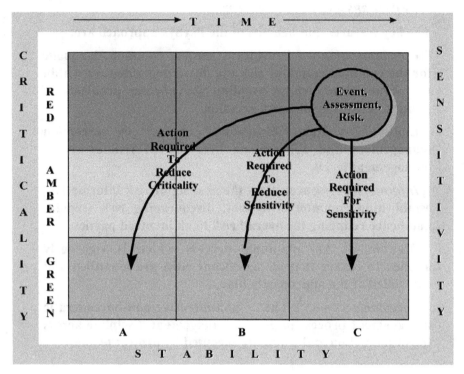

Project Criticality, Stability and Sensitivity: Measures To Be Taken To Reduce The Risk Impact

The core of *I.T. Risk Management* is the Assessment Analysis. This uses structured techniques to analyse project plans and identify the most sensitive events that are potentially unstable, and therefore the source of greatest risk.

Everything is rated on a GAR principle: **G**reen, **A**mber and **R**ed scale; where G is always 'good' and R is always 'bad'. This provides an instantly understood assessment on each stage: Events, Assessments, and Risks in relationship with the time scales as used in the plans. This, effectively, provides guidance on how best to attack the risk.

3.6 STRATEGIC COST ANALYSIS

Costing is a process within *I.T. Risk Management* that can be used to define the cost of risk within a project or business area from as early as the proposal stage. It works by adding a 'quality' dimension to the estimating process so that high quality estimates, based on relevant experience, are treated differently from low quality estimates which are little more than guesses.

The output takes the form of a probability distribution diagram and a set of assessments which need to be managed in order to move the curve to the left and squeeze it (i.e. reduce the likely cost and the uncertainty).

Costing is particularly useful in the early stages of a project when the final cost of the project is subject to great uncertainty. The process has also been effectively used to define business budgets for re-structured business areas.

3.7 RISK ADMINISTRATION SYSTEM TOOL

A Microsoft Access based tool or any type of an ordinary spreadsheet can be utilised to allow the events, assessments, and risks to be captured and reviewed by all stockholders in the program. In this way risks that would have been missed are captured through the identification of events.

3.8 WORK PLAN ANALYSIS

Work Plan Analysis is a set of techniques that enables a rapid risk assessment to be undertaken on a complex project which is already in progress.

It is always difficult to focus on the right areas when the project organisation is large and the plans are extensive and likely to be multi-levelled. Using Work Plan Analysis, the 'poor quality' areas of a project are quickly highlighted for further investigation.

One very successful application of this approach has been through the use of Project Readiness Assessment Walkthroughs. These are structured review meetings held just prior to major project milestones or deliverables. Initially the project team explain their self-evaluation of the project status and are questioned by an independent review team. Potential risks arising are captured using the Assessment Analysis process.

3.9 COMMUNICATING THE RISKS

The I.T. Risk Management techniques summarised above will only deliver its full benefits to any business if a suitable governance structure is quickly established to communicate the risk information and set suitable actions to mitigate the risks. The mapping of the process onto an organisation is the key step to ensuring that the investment in the *I.T. Risk Management* process is fully realised.

4 PRINCIPLES OF RISK MANAGEMENT

4.1 TEAM APPROACH

An enterprise must escape from a culture based on transfer of risk between parties, to a team approach that is focused on attacking the real source of the risks. Methods must be effective without the need for detailed, time consuming analysis.

4.2 DEFINITION OF A RISK

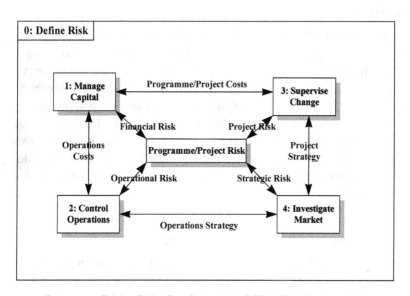

Programme/Project Risk: One Component Of The Total Business Risk.

A risk may be perceived as a possible loss. Risk is individual to a person or organisation because - what is perceived by one individual as a major risk may be perceived by another as a minor risk.

A risk is linked very strongly with competitiveness. Each decision has the possibility of resulting in loss. Each decision to introduce a new product into the marketplace can result in varying degrees of loss or gain. To be entrepreneurial is to accept risk, that is, the possibility of loss. A good entrepreneur's strength, however, is to make decisions which maximise possible gain. Hence minimise possible loss, which constitutes effective risk management.

Risk is inherent in all aspect of an organisation and may be viewed from four primary directions: financial, operational, programme/project and portfolio/products. Many risks are related to the running of the operations and its processes but is often in trying to change operations that the greatest risk is experienced. It is the management of risk in such 'change' projects that the I.T. Risk Management methodology addresses.

A project can be described in its simplest terms as: Planning to achieve specific objectives and then executing the plans. The emphasis is on the word 'plan' as without a plan we have no project. So in the context of a project, a risk is something which might disrupt the plans such that the objectives of the project are not met. The discipline of Project Risk Management is thus a framework of techniques which allows the project manager to pro-actively identify and manage risks before they develop into problems which will impact the project plans.

4.3 APPROACHES TO RISK MANAGEMENT

In recent years we have seen large projects in many areas of business suffering from a lack of control. The size of cost and time over-runs do not seem to be decreasing, despite the amount of management time which is being dedicated to analysing and quantifying the potential problems and selecting suitable personnel and processes. One may conclude that management, either do not have the correct methods and tools in place to attack the potential problems, or that they are not using, or do not understand, those which they do have.

In the early 1970's, the concepts of formal project risk management began to emerge. Hailed as the saviour of project managers, in practice the results have been mixed. Risk management has proved highly effective in certain mature industries - e.g. the Petrochemical or construction industry where project managers can base their estimates on years of similar engineering experience. Difficulties seem to be encountered when these traditional Risk Management methods are applied to innovative and fast evolving areas such as Information Technology.

4.4 EVENTS AND RISK REGISTERS

Most projects will have an Events Register and some may have what they call a Risk Register. In effect, this tends to be a list into which anyone can input their concerns. It will contain references to current problems, questions, and assessments, difficult activities about which there is reasonable confidence and the odd real risk.

In any large project the Events or Risk Register quickly becomes swamped with items that require very different actions and many which do not require any action at all. All this leads to an inevitable loss of focus. Further, the content tends to be biased towards current problems rather than future potential problems.

4.5 INDIVIDUAL INTERVIEWS

One-on-one interviews can be an effective way of capturing risks. When people are not inhibited by management and peers, they tend to be far more open about their concerns. Unfortunately, most use much unsophisticated approaches such as "what do you see as your risks?" or "what keeps you awake at night?" Thus, if the person interviewed is sensitive to discussing risks it may prevent the capture of any valuable information. At best the risks captured will tend to lack structure as they are not focused onto the future objectives that the project plans to achieve.

4.6 GROUP BRAINSTORMING

Group brainstorming can be a very effective technique for opening up a very complex situation. However, information can be subconsciously suppressed by peer pressure, which may bias the discussion on one area at the expense of the rest of the project. Inevitably the mass of information captured is often difficult to focus, prioritise, and allocate ownership.

In general, it should be remembered that the quality of the output is only as good as the quality of the input data.

4.7 RISK ANALYSIS AND QUANTIFICATION

Risks may be difficult to capture reliably and concisely but further problems are likely to be experienced when trying to analyse them. Virtually all approaches to risk analysis are based on estimating the factored impact of the risk. This exposure to risk is a combination of the chance (probability) of an event happening and the consequences (impact) if it does occur i.e.

Risk Exposure = Potential Impact x Probability of Occurrence

Fundamental problems arise when individuals are required to estimate, numerically, the impact and then predict (numerically) the probability. Estimates, which are often little more than guesses, result in a single point estimate of Risk Exposure, which is then given undeserved credibility in the detailed analysis of the risk and used as the basis for many major project decisions. Also, it is often the case that part of the risk impact can be quantified but often not the major part. An example can be based on an attempt to quantify bad publicity, quality, and relationship.

Some processes add complexity by rating the impact of risks in terms of financial, time scales, quality, performance etc., which quickly become very tedious to maintain.

4.8 RISK CONTROL AND FOLLOW-THROUGH

Many risk management systems fail due to a lack of follow-through on actions. There is a surprising tendency to identify risks and then watch them happen!

This is caused by:

☐ Failure to use the risk register to set appropriate action plans,

☐ Lack of regular updates/maintenance of the risk register,

☐ Absence of named owners and deadlines (lack of ownership),

☐ Tracking generalities rather than specifics,

☐ Concentrating on what can be done if the risk occurs rather than stopping the risk happening (pro-active),

☐ Trying to transfer the risk elsewhere, without considering the consequences.

4.9 RISK TRANSFER

Risk transfer often occurs because the partner who knows most about the level of risk within the enterprise (i.e. the supplier/purchaser relationship) is encouraged to transfer this to the other partner. Once accomplished, the party with the most knowledge of the risk relaxes and the most ignorant partner inherits the risk. An example of this is the Purchaser insisting on a fixed-price contract in a poorly defined contract when they know that the supplier does not understand the scope of the contract.

The supplier then has a tendency to deliver the minimum possible and obtain sign-off for everything, irrespective of quality. The effect of this type of commercial 'table-tennis' is actually to increase the level of risk within the enterprise as the real risks pile up without intervention.

What is needed is a method that identifies and encourages the attack of real risk at source. Such a method would force projects within the enterprise to become pro-active by attacking risks, rather than waiting for events to unfold and then counting the cost, as recorded in the previous month's financial returns.

4.10 RISK AND PROJECT MANAGEMENT

There is often a tendency to treat risk management as no more than another necessary evil of project management. Thus, it often becomes an additional administrative burden for the Project Manager and consequently does not get the quality attention to make it work effectively.

In order to make risk management work, a shift in philosophy is required. This must lead the project team to view the process not just as another component of project management, but more as the communication stabiliser that holds the project together.

5. PRINCIPLES OF RISK METHODOLOGY

5.1 PROCESS

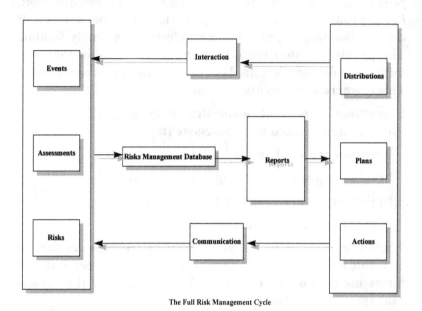

The Full Risk Management Cycle

The *I.T. Risk Management* method described in this book aims to provide an effective means of managing risks within all types of projects. The *I.T. Risk Management* process grew out of a thorough assessment of the problems often encountered in project management and the techniques of the traditional risk management approaches that have been used to try and improve the situation.

Both good and bad principles were noted and new techniques were introduced to address key deficiencies. The resulting *I.T. Risk Management* process has a proven track record of delivering tangible results in large projects across a diverse range of organisations.

5.2 COMMUNICATION OF ASSESSMENTS

As already highlighted, a fundamental reason for project failure is the lack of quality communications both within the project and between the programme and its environment. Most problems incurred by projects could be avoided if information was effectively communicated in a timely fashion. The problem is that there is so much information that it is difficult to decide what needs to be communicated and to who. This is where assessments come in.

Everything important associated with a project can be captured and tracked as an assessment:

☐ Activities are sized on the basis of assessments,

☐ Milestones are set according to assessments,

☐ Dependencies are based on assessments,

☐ Plans are executed by making assessments.

Therefore, the capture, analysis, and communication of assessments are critical to the success of any project, and this forms the core of the I.T. Risk Management and the Project Management process.

5.3 CURRENT PROJECT PLAN - BASELINE

Risks are identified by capturing the critical assessments in the project plans are uncertain. In other words, whatever might stop the objectives, timescales, and budget of the project plan being ach Both good and bad principles were noted and new techniques were introduced to address key deficiencies. The resulting *I.T. Risk Management* process has a proven track record of delivering tangible results in large projects across a diverse ieved. In this way, all assessments are effectively referenced to the project plans. Consequently, the plan provides the focus for the risk management process.

This approach keeps the risks specific, forward looking and ensures that the plan is always sufficiently detailed and up to date.

5.4 UNCERTAINTY EQUALS RISK

Risk is inherent whenever there is uncertainty. The best judges of uncertainty are those who are asked to make estimates for the plans and, in most circumstances, the people who will actually have to do the work make the best estimators.

Combining this principle with the assessments captured from the project plans leads us to rate assessments for quality/uncertainty. Analysis is concentrated onto the areas of the project about which little is known and particularly the inter-dependencies that often represent the highest risk.

5.5 QUALITY JUDGEMENT SCALE

To capture this vital information about how sure the estimator is, each estimator is asked, not only for assessments

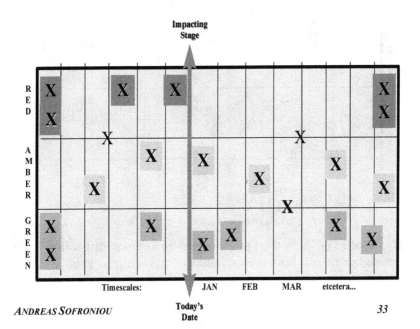

or the value of any estimate, but also, what quality he or she considers the assessment or estimate to be. This is not a judgement of the skill of the estimator. It is a self-assessment of the current quality of the basic information, upon which the project plans are based.

The risks scale is defined for multiple uses throughout the process. It always means effectively the same thing i.e. A is always good and C is always bad. B expresses tendencies to the two extremes.

☐ A (Green) means very good, high confidence, not important

☐ B (Amber) means fairly good, reasonable confidence, not very important

☐ C (Red) means very poor, little or no confidence, and critically important.

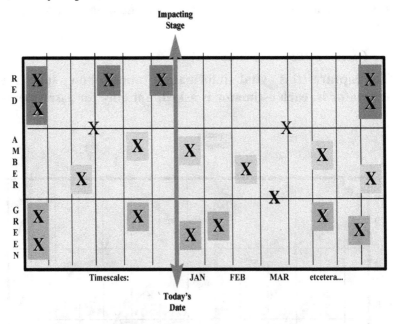

Impacting Risks

It should be noted that the method does not allow the estimator to say that the estimate or assessment is of average quality. The whole principle is that we should be forced to make a choice between good, high confidence and bad, low confidence estimates and cannot 'sit on the fence'.

Using these simple A, B, C terms to express degrees of uncertainty, it is possible to encourage the estimator to reveal a wide range of uncertainty. Also, it is often possible to persuade him or her to make estimates when not normally prepared to do so. Being able to qualify an assessment or estimate with a C quality, often assures the estimators that they will not be forced into a given value or statement. We can thus gain vital information about the uncertainty and therefore the risks that may lie at the heart of the project without even asking for a risk.

5.6 PROCESS OVERVIEW

The *I.T. Risk Management* process consists of an integrated closed loop method, which logically progresses through:

☐ Project Prioritisation (for multiple project environments),

☐ Risk Assessment (consisting of Assessments Analysis plus Strategic Cost Analysis and/or Work Plan Analysis, if appropriate),

☐ Risk Prioritisation (to decide the 'order of attack'),

☐ Risk Control (to put the mitigation plans into action and monitor their effectiveness).

5.7 PROJECT PRIORITISATION

A large organisation may have, at any one time, hundreds of projects of varying size, and nature. Yet many organisations have no formal mechanism for prioritising projects leading to problems such as:

☐ Not knowing which projects should be approved/resourced,

☐ Uncertainty as to which projects should be formally assessed for risk.

Once the critical and potentially risky projects have been identified, I.T. Risk Management offers three risk assessment techniques to identify and analyse the specific risks within each project.

The Assumption Analysis technique provides a backbone onto which the Strategic Cost Analysis and/or Work Plan Analysis approaches can be built.

In this respect Assumption Analysis would always be applied, Strategic Cost Analysis would be used in the early stages of a project or proposal to address the uncertainty in the cost/pricing of the project and Work Plan Analysis may be used to assess a very complex project which is well progressed.

5.8 RISK PRIORITISATION

The specific risks captured from each project risk assessment needs to be prioritised in order to allocate resources and decide the order in which the risks should be addressed.

The method provides a simple framework which rates each risk for Criticality, Controllability, and Impact Timing. The resulting list of risks is captured in a Microsoft Access Risk Register (or any type of spreadsheet) and the risks are summarised in a diagram which provides an executive overview of the project risk profile.

The diagram shown in *8.5* can also be used in this stage, as this can be modified to include the list of impacting risks as reported by the Risk Register. Although this figure shows risks with the letter X, in reality, the Xs can be replaced by the actual system generated risks reports.

5.9 RISK CONTROL

This provides a framework for risk control based on taking both strategic and tactical views of attacking risks. The strategic approach is achieved by applying trend analysis to the underlying assessments to identify any strong Risk Drivers, which can be neutralised together.

Tactical approaches match the complexity of the risk action plan to the complexity of the risk to minimise bureaucracy for simple-to-manage risks, whilst maintaining the necessary formality for complex risks.

The purpose of the diagram below is to show to the reader that at a certain point of time, measures have to be taken to reduce the impact of a Critical, Unstable and/or a Sensitive event, assessment and/or risk.

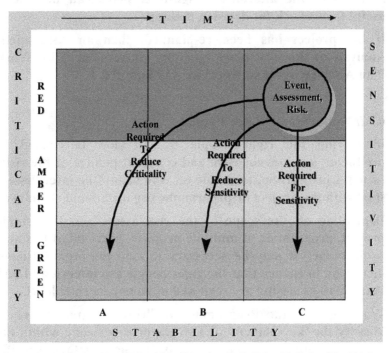

Project Criticality, Stability and Sensitivity: Measures To Be Taken To Reduce The Risk Impact

6 PROJECT IN TROUBLE

6.1 RE-PLANNING

The key aspect of a project in trouble is that it requires re-planning to put it back on track. Thus, the timing of the risk assessment relative to this planning process is very important.

If the re-planning process has not started there will be very little of the new approach to assess. It may be possible to influence this new approach by undertaking a risk assessment of the options being considered. To do this an Assumption Analysis of the alternative high-level plans can provide a useful framework for decision making.

If the project has been re-planned, then an Assessment Analysis of the new plans, possibly supplemented by Work Plan Analysis, is an appropriate way forward.

6.2 INTERVIEWS WITH KEY PEOPLE

Identifying the right people to interview is critical to producing a comprehensive and coherent picture of the risks facing a project. So, to decide on who should be interviewed, start with the project or programme organisational structure.

Depending on the scope of the risk assessment (i.e. single project, programme of multiple projects, portfolio of business projects etc.) it may be necessary to map the organisational hierarchy to ensure that the right people are interviewed and that the risks arising are reviewed at an appropriate level.

Working with the Programme or Project Manager, try to identify the 'key players'. A key player is someone within the programme/project who is likely to have either specific expertise in a particular area and/or insight into the environment in which the project is being implemented.

Key players tend to be Project Managers for a programme or Team Managers for a project with the addition of Users involved in the requirement capture and other activities. This group would likely form the initial interview list.

During the interview, these people should decide who else they need to participate. Interviewers need to exercise their judgement when evaluating the responses to this question. Typically it is necessary to go down at least one level below the Project/Team manager unless the team size is small.

One of the key features of the I.T. Risk Management process is that of obtaining counter viewpoints within the organisation. Thus, the more people that are interviewed, the better. However, if many projects are being assessed for risk within an organisation, resource constraints will inevitably lead to reducing the interview pool. Under these circumstances at least two counter viewpoints must be obtained within each project. (e.g.: business manager and technical manager) so that the assessment ratings can be compared.

6.3 CHOOSING RISK ASSESSMENT TEAM

The team that will operate and manage the I.T. Risk Management process requires a particular set of skills and background to be successful:

☐ Experience of working in large (preferably non-consulting) projects and managing (preferably) medium sized projects (say 10-20 people).

☐ Understanding of project planning principles and some exposure to associated tools.

☐ Forceful personalities to ensure quality data captures in difficult client situations.

☐ IT background, in order to understand the issues in IT projects and to help with using the I.T. Risk Management support tools.

☐ Some understanding of the clients business.

Note that it can sometimes be a disadvantage to have too much knowledge of the clients business in applying the I.T. Risk Management process. This is because there may be a tendency for the interviewer to get into too much detail in non-risky areas and take too much of the client's time in the process.

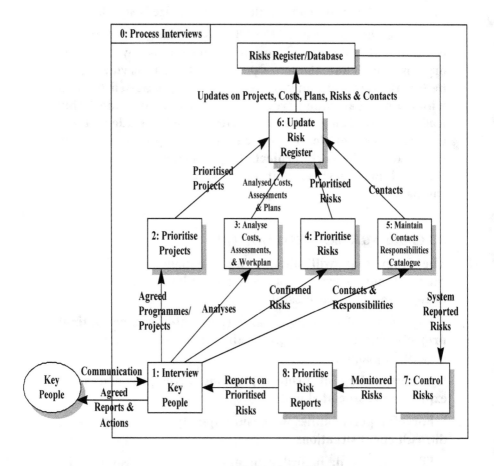

The Interviewing Process

6.4 RISK REVIEW MEETINGS

After the initial round of interviews, a suitable forum must be established to discuss the risks identified. The client may suggest that the risks are discussed as part of the regular project meeting. This should be resisted unless the risks are an early agenda item and there will be sufficient time to get through the agenda with this additional discussion.

Typically, a minimum of an hour will be required for discussion of the risks - all if possible but just the most critical if not. If discussion of the risks is left to the end there will often be little time (or concentration) left to do the process justice. Also, it is likely that some events will end up being discussed twice. If discussed first, the risks tend to focus the meeting and get away from talking about progress onto the things that need to be discussed - i.e. what threatens the success of the project.

The best method is to establish a specific Risk Review Meeting with a representation consisting of the Risk Owners and chaired by the Programme Director, or the process 'champion' in the client organisation.

6.5 PROJECT PRIORITISATION PROCESS

In order to help refine the appropriate positioning of projects, each business area must identify two or three current key projects with which management are familiar. After agreement between the senior client and supplier managers, these will be positioned to make up a standard reference matrix. This matrix will then be used as the baseline.

6.6 POSITIONING NEW PROJECTS

Initial positioning of the new project should be undertaken by the supplier and client project managers, together, as early as possible in the project. Complete consensus is not always possible at this stage, due to incomplete understanding of the business and technical issues involved.

However, it is essential that consensus is reached before any approval boards, or it is clear that the project is not ready to proceed. Lack of consensus can result in biased project ratings. Too high a rating will waste resources and cause frustration within the project team due to excessive management attention. Too low a rating will result in management neglect and consequently, increased risk.

6.7 PROJECT APPROVAL AND RESOURCES

In practice, the primary factor that is taken into consideration when approving a project is the Business Criticality. There are many projects that could be undertaken and only a finite resource pool available, so only the projects that will most improve the organisation's business should be approved.

Once management endorsement has been obtained, the results of the positioning exercise should be published to the teams and senior management.

6.8 PROJECTS CHANGE ON DIAGRAM

Once a project has been positioned it will be subject to review at least once every phase and certainly before progressing to the next stage. The most significant event in the life of a project is likely to be if it moves within either matrix.

A project may move because it is discovered that it is more or less complex than previously thought. It may have grown or been reduced in size. It may have become more or less critical to the client's business.

If a project moves, it is indicating something about the management approach required in the future. In particular, the approach to risk management should be reviewed and projects moving towards the top-right corner of the matrix should be assessed whilst projects moving towards the bottom left corner may be dropped from the risk assessment process.

6.9 RISK MANAGEMENT DECISION

The position of a project on the diagram is also used to determine which projects should be assessed formally for risk going forward. The threshold can be set at any appropriate level. For example, some organisations work on the principle that any project judged to be a C, on either matrix, should be assessed for risk using the I.T. Risk Management process. Projects falling below this threshold are still encouraged to use a formal method for risk assessment, but it is not mandated.

6.10 RISK IDENTIFICATION AND ANALYSIS

The risk method uses three windows; Assessment Analysis, Strategic Cost Analysis and Work Plan Analysis, to obtain a clear view of the source of any risk.

Although it is possible to create risk by poor planning and management, an element of risk is inherent in any enterprise. The main problem is to find a method of identifying the sources of the risks in time to allow specific actions to be taken to avoid or reduce the impact.

The nature of the project risks varies with the nature of the tasks, the size and the development phase of the project. Later phases may make use of methods for identifying risk based on the project's experiences to date. In early phases, good quality information and experience is scarce. Thus, different phases and different types of risk are best looked at by using different techniques and tools.

By using all these windows over the life of a project we increase our chances of identifying the major risks which lie within the project and to understand the nature of each risk.

The process ultimately allows us to represent each risk in terms of:

☐ The potential criticality of the risk in terms of impact on the core project objectives,

☐ The point in time that the risk will impact the project if unresolved,

☐ The likelihood of the risk occurring.

Using these three analysis techniques; Strategic Cost Analysis, Assessment Analysis and Work Plan Analysis, it is possible to generate a single list that contains all the fundamental risks to the project. This list can then be used to decide which elements represent important risks and should thus be subject to proactive Risk Management by the creation and execution of dedicated Risk Plans.

7 COMMUNICATING RISKS

7.1 PRESENTATION

Communicating risks to senior management groups is always difficult as they are often not familiar with the detail of the project. Subsequently, the risks need to be presented in a concise, clear way which explains what is causing the risk (and therefore indicates what needs to be done) and what would be the consequences if the risk is allowed to impact the project.

Thus assessments are converted into risks using the form:

If (the assessment proves incorrect),

Then (describe the consequences to the project or business).

It is important to express the full consequences of the risk or it may fail the "so-what", test when submitted to senior management. A good principle is to describe at least the immediate impact and the ultimate impact on the project programme or business.

An alternative representation of a risk is to leave the assessments stated in the positive and add the impact. The advantage of this is that the risk can still be expressed in a positive sense. Some people find this very important.

7.2 CATEGORISATION OF ASSESSMENTS

When capturing assessments, it is often useful to identify what is driving the Sensitivity and Stability ratings allocated to it so that the source (or "driver" of the risk) is clear. This is simply achieved by categorising assessments into one of three types:

☐ Policy where the assessment relates to a business decision or policy, standards, resourcing priorities etc. The assessment requires management intervention to bring it under control.

☐ Milestone where the timescales of the activities are being 'squeezed' or timescale dependencies on other projects, suppliers etc. The assessment would be no problem if more time were available.

☐ Technical where the complexity of the undertaking is driving the ratings (e.g. untried design, hardware and software constraints, complex organisations etc.). The complexity is such that mistakes are likely irrespective of the time available.

Categorising assessments in this way can make the selection of appropriate Risk Plans easier by ensuring that the true source of the risk is addressed. Further, it can allow a strategic view of the risks to be obtained but only when a statistically large number of risks are being tracked.

7.3 PROJECT READINESS WALKTHROUGHS

Project Readiness Walkthroughs are a highly effective way of ensuring that all risks have been captured from the assessments analysis process. When used independently from, or prior to, an Assessments Analysis, the walkthrough provides a start to the risk assessment process which is particularly useful when time is short.

Project walkthrough:

☐ Assess the readiness to meet milestones for high-priority projects,

☐ Identify any corporate resource contention that may exist, and assist with prioritisation,

☐ Identify common events and risks, and communicate information to support other project teams,

☐ Help project teams achieve their goals by identifying and/or providing resources for assistance as needed,

☐ Assess enterprise-wide risk through the evaluation of multiple projects.

The walkthrough is completed by going through the As and Bs and asking for them to be (briefly) justified. Any additional assessments or risks are logged.

The matrix is updated to reflect the risks identified to produce an exit matrix.

The risks reviewed regularly and actions stated to ensure that they are brought under control.

7.4 ASSESSMENTS AND RISKS REGISTER

All assessments captured should be held in an Assessments Register. Only critical assessments will be converted into risks and held in a Risk Register. This is done by filtering the assessments and consolidating them into risks. All information captured will be rationalised and details of their source and consequences will be traceable.

7.5 POSITIONING RISKS

In certain instances the risk may undermine the basic objectives of the project and no amount of money will save the project if such a risk impacts. If not resolved, the uncertainty may halt the progress of the project. Such a risk may be related to the overall programme, a part of the programme, an individual part of the design, or even a particular module of software. This, also, provides a way of representing the effect of such risks on the overall project, where cost impact is small or meaningless.

The timing of a risk should always equate to the latest time to start the first necessary action. In this respect, it is analogous with trying to stop a cancer. This must be done at the point that it starts to grow, not when it can be first being seen.

7.6 RISK REGISTER REPORTS

Impact Diagrams provide an overview or risk profile of the project. However, the detail of the risks is required for the risk review meeting in order that the detail of the risks can be seen, discussed and actions taken.

The order of the risks in the report is important so that senior management can focus on the key risks first.

If the impact diagram is used to prioritise the risk register the time element can be easily included. For instance there may be an urgent AMBER criticality, C controllability risk that needs attention that is not an obvious priority if the Risk Report is prioritised by Criticality and Controllability alone.

In essence the easiest way to prioritise is to use the Impact Diagram and to treat the highest priority risk as the one nearest to the origin, the next nearest being number two and so on. The intention is to order the risks so that they are roughly in the right order.

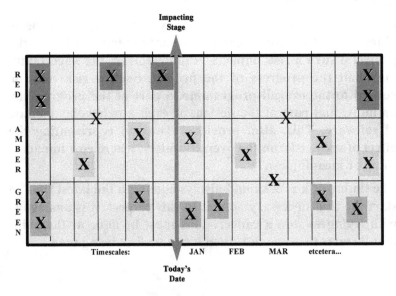

Impacting Risks

7.7 RISK PLANS REQUIREMENTS

Risks which cannot be resolved by improved planning must be tackled individually through the use of dedicated Risk Plans. Ultimately, the plans for reducing the risks must be incorporated into the main project plans.

Risk Plans may be divided into "Simple" or "Complex", irrespective of the potential impact of the risk. Simple means that it is possible to resolve the risk quickly say by a simple phone call or single task. For such risks, monitoring the status on the Risk Report is sufficient and minimises bureaucracy. Complex risks require significant resources and time to resolve them and for these a formal Risk Plan is required.

7.8 COMPONENTS OF A FORMAL RISK PLAN

For complex risks, it is essential that a structured plan is formulated. This will clarify thinking, provide the necessary visibility, and feed directly into the main planning process:

The basic components of a Risk Plan are:

☐ The risk statement and its ratings,

☐ Risk Owner and Risk Action Manager,

☐ The driving statement and its ratings,

☐ Assessment Originator,

☐ Objectives of the Risk Plan i.e. Stabilise the assessment,

☐ Criteria i.e. how will we know when the objectives have been met,

☐ Risk Plan summary i.e. what are the steps to meet the objectives,

☐ Reference to project plans,

☐ Additional resources required,

☐ Monitoring process i.e. how often and by whom,

☐ Re-assessment of the driving assessment (completed after execution of the Risk Plan)

☐ Fall-back plans i.e. what we do if the Risk Plan fails.

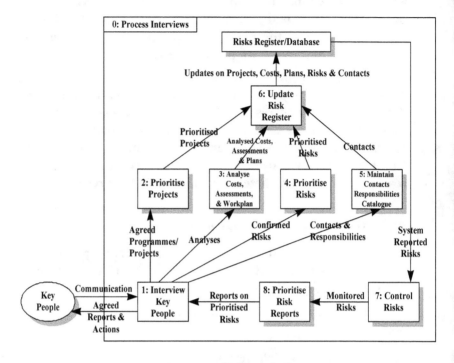

The Interviewing Process

8 METHODOLOGIES

8.1 INTEGRATING METHODOLOGIES

In handing over and in applying any Risk Management method, as in any other Management tool, the integration of all existing methodologies is of primary importance.

In choosing the new owner of the I.T. Risk Management methodology, consideration must be given regarding the experience possessed by the new proprietor. Preference should be given to the people with systems methodology and management procedures training and experience.

The diagram below will serve as a guide on what the knowledge should include.

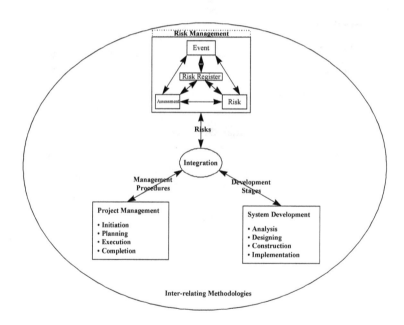

8.2 *INTEGRATION*

The diagrammatic flow shown below is the desired overall integration of related top-level processes:

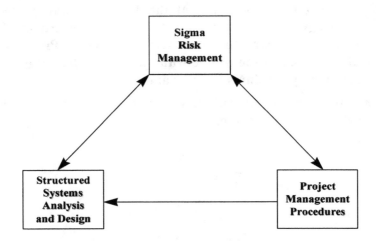

Integration Of Methodologies

8.3 SUGGESTED INTERFACING

The suggested interfacing of the Structured Systems Analysis and Design methodology and the Project Management procedures to the Risk Management processes may be done separately as shown in the diagram below:

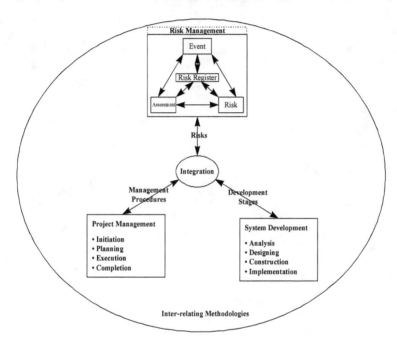

9. MANAGING THE RISK PROGRAMME

9.1 DIAGRAMMATIC REPRESENTATION

The term *'Sigma'* used in the process boxes in some diagrams below is based on the PsySys method of Risk Management.

9.2 RISK MANAGEMENT DECOMPOSITION

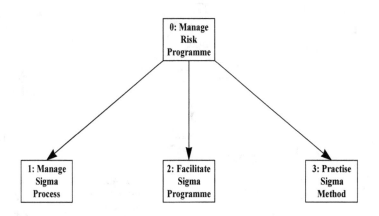

The Sigma Risk Management Decomposition

9.3 RISK PROGRAMME MANAGEMENT

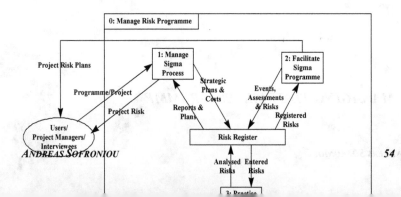

9.4 *MANAGING THE RISK PROCESS*

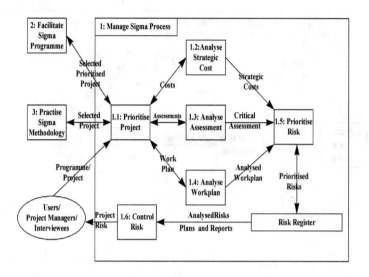

9.5 *Facilitation of Risk Programme*

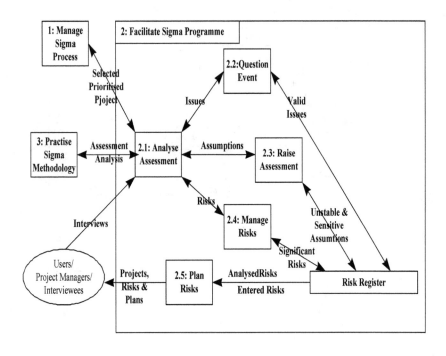

9.6 PRACTISING RISK METHODOLOGY

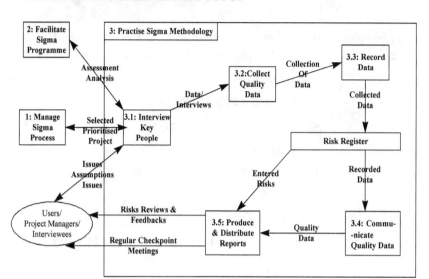

9.7 DATAFLOW DIAGRAMS RELATIONSHIP

All dataflow diagrams shown in above pages are based on the PsySys Limited manuals and handouts as used for the Risk Management training.

DATAFLOW DIAGRAMS:	DESCRIPTION OF DIAGRAMS AND THEIR PROCESSES.
0: Manage Risk Programme	Project: something complex that you want (plan) to happen.
	Risk: Something that you don't want to happen.
	Project management: Planning and making things happen.
	Risk management: Attacking anything that

	might disturb the plans
1: Manage I.T. Risk Management Process	The Risk Management process consists of an integrated closed loop method which logically progresses through: • Project Prioritisation, • Strategic Cost Analysis, • Assessment Analysis, • Work Plan Analysis, • Risk Prioritisation, • Risk Control.
1.1 Prioritise Project	Only complex and critical projects need to have a fully structured risk management process in place.
1.2 Analyse Strategic Cost	Strategic Cost Analysis provides a means of assessing the cost risk in a project in its very early stages and "kick-starts" the risk management process.
1.3 Analyse Assessment	Fundamentally, projects only fail due to two reasons either the wrong assumptions were made or the significance of the assumptions was not understood.
1.4 Analyse Work plan	Work Plan Analysis may be used to focus on the risky areas of detailed, multi-level project plans when time is of the essence.
1.5 Prioritise Risk	Prioritisation allows the Project Manager to divert limited resources at the most critical project risk.
1.6 Control Risk	Risks may be attacked at both the strategic and tactical levels. Strategic approaches look for trends and underlying causes for groups of risks. Tactical approaches take each risk at

	face value.
2: Facilitate Programme	The Risk Management Programme is essentially a framework process that allows the capture of collective knowledge and viewpoints from those involved on the project, in a form that facilitates communication of events, assessments and ensures pro-active management of risks. By dramatically improving communication, risks are avoided or managed proactively and project objectives are delivered on time.
2.1: Analyse Assessment	The core of the Risk Management is the Assessment Analysis. This uses structured techniques to analyse project plans and identify the most sensitive assumptions that are potentially unstable, and therefore the source of greatest risk.
2.2: Question Event	Events are open questions which are holding up plans/implementation. An Event is any open question which has been asked at the right time to which a high quality answer cannot be provided without escalation.
2.3: Raise Assessment	Many Events are closed by making Assessments in plans. An Assessment is a single, simple, positive, or negative statement.
2.4: Manage Risks	Unstable/sensitive assumptions create risks. Significant risks need to be managed formally. Definition: A Risk is a simple statement of the form: "IF" Assumption proves incorrect, "THEN"

	Describe the impact.
2.5: Plan Risks	Risk Plans impact project plans.
	Events, Assessments, and risks are inherent in the project plans.
	Population of assessment and risks registers by progressing Risk Plans/Main/Project Plans.
3: Practise Risk Methodology	The Role of a Risk Management Practitioner includes:
	Interview 'Key People' within the project,
	To collect 'Quality' data,
	Ensure the data collected is recorded in the Risk Register,
	Communicate the 'Quality' data to Project staff,
	Produces accurate and timely reports for meetings:
	Weekly Check Point Meetings,
	Risk Review Boards.
3.1: Interview Key People	Identifying the right people to interview is critical to producing a comprehensive and coherent picture of the risks facing a project. So, to decide who should be interviewed, start with the project or programme organisational structure. Depending on the scope of the risk assessment it may be necessary to map the organisational hierarchy to ensure that the right people are interviewed and that the risks arising are reviewed at an appropriate level.
3.2: Collect Quality Data	This function requires to:

	Interview 'Key People' within the project, Collect 'Quality' data.
3.3: Record Data	Having Interviewed the 'Key People' within the project and collected the 'Quality' data: Ensure the data collected is recorded in the Risk Register.
3.4: Communicate Quality Data	The interviews of 'Key People' within the project have been completed, the 'Quality' data recorded in the Risk Register and communicated to Project staff, the next function is: Facilitate and ensure the Risk Management process stays on track.
3.5: Produce Reports	After the initial round of interviews, a suitable forum must be established to discuss the risks identified. The best method is to establish a specific Risk Review Meeting with a representation consisting of the Risk Owners and chaired by the Programme Director or the process 'champion' in the client organisation. The main function is to: • Produce accurate and timely reports for meetings, • Weekly Check Point Meetings, • Risk Review Boards.

Detester/Database Of Events, Assessments, and Risks Register Description.

Data Store: **Risk Register**	All events, assessments, and risks captured should be held in a Risks Register. Remember, only critical assessments will be converted into risks and held in a Risk Register. Thus, by filtering the assessments and consolidating them into risks, all information captured will be rationalised and details of their source and consequences will be traceable.

10 PROJECT MANAGEMENT IMPROVEMENTS

10.1 PROJECT MANAGEMENT WEAKNESS

In the process of using I.T. Risk Management, it will soon become apparent that probably the main cause for the threatening risks is project management, or perhaps the weakness of individual/s to manage the growth of a system.

Even if you used I.T. Risk Management in its fullest, your experience will soon enable you to identify the real cause for the failure in implementing your system. In such cases, your programme/project management may need further support, assistance, training, better communicational ability and proper delegating, or even some listening to other people involved in the on-going project. Employing the expertise of a consultancy may help.

 The main point is to try to reduce potential project caused loss by providing efficient *Event* driven project reviews for the critical project/s. Such project consulting steps will create and utilise virtual group of experienced project managers. As a panel of experts they will assess critical projects and provide consulting being perceived as helpful by the project team, the management, and the users/clients.

10.2 PROCESS STEPS

For such a project consulting programme implementation, various process steps are needed:

1. Select critical project,

2. Understand project status,

3. Plan project review,

4. Create reviews agenda

5. Execute project review,

6. Implement change plan,

7. Conclude the project review.

10.3 INFORMATION COLLECTION

The project manager of the project pending the review should gather the requested information from the existing project documentation. If such documentation is not available, the project manager should collect as much as possible from verbal discussions.

Such a preparation should include details of:

1. Communication plans,
2. Project organisation plan,
3. Contacts and scopes,
4. Background and status of finances,
5. Schedules,
6. Status and history of resources plans,
7. Quality plan,
8. System documentation,
9. Brief description of the project environment,
10. Risk register prioritisation/s and other reports,
11. Last project review minutes.

10.4 RESOURCES AGREEMENT

The final outcome of all communications, discussions and reviews should enable the team members to produce an agreed score on the various project management resources.

The list for such a scoring agreement should include:

1. Quality management,
2. User participation,
3. Requirements management,
4. Communications,
5. Business orientation,
6. Project team,

7. Project planning,

8. Risk management,

9. Technical environment.

10.5 *SCORE GRAPH*

A scoring card graph can easily be produced on a spreadsheet and it ought to look something like this:

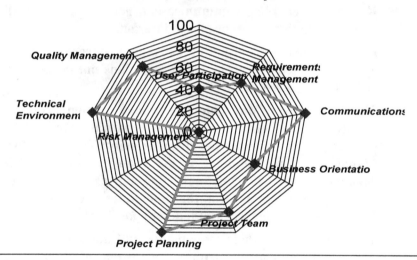

11. I.T. RISKS LOGICAL ANALYSIS POINTS

A risk is an uncertain event which may have an adverse effect on the project's objectives. This Risk Management book is based on a proven risk management methodology, which should be very effective in the quest for identifying risks throughout the project life-cycle.

Remember, this I.T. Risk Management methodology is:

• Forward looking, investigating problems and how to deal with threats,

• A tool enabling communication, getting people at all levels to talk to each other and to interact,

• A no blame team culture, bringing concerns into the open where actions can be taken and plans put in place, in order to stop a risk occurring.

The I.T. Risk Management process commences by identifying the enterprises most important and risky projects, as these must be given priority. This I.T. Risk Management book/manual is essentially a method that permits the collection of knowledge and experience from those involved, in a form that facilitates the Systematic Interaction and Generic Methodology for Applications.

The varied events, their assessments, and the consequential risks relating to or consisting of a system. Methodical in procedures and plans, these are addressed to those involved and deliberating within the parameters of their systems development responsibilities.

The results will depend on interaction. The mutual or reciprocal action which encourages those involved in the programmes and projects to communicate with each other and to work closely with a view to solving the threatening events before they impact on the development of the system. The individuals involved maintain a generic approach, which relates and characterises the whole group of those involved in assessing the events and attacking the threatening ones before they become risks to the development of the system.

The end result being the avoidance of apparent problems within the pre-defined users' systems requirements. This is enabled by following the Risk Management Methodology. The system architects and the risk management practitioners simply follow the approved body of systems development methods, rules and management procedures employed by their organisation. For practical or even ethical reasons, it must be noted that with such a philosophy, it is seldom possible to fulfil all requirements of very large organisational systems.

As such, the risk methodology is administered in applications. Putting to use such techniques and in applying the risk management principles in the development of various applications will involve numerous and varied activities. A concrete issue in developing new applications is the problem of communication among the people involved, the motivation constantly needed for generic work, the ability to interact systematically and in using a structured systems methodology.

END

INDEX OF CONTENTS: PAGE:

BIBLIOGRAPHY:

I.T. RISK MANAGEMENT – 2011 EDITION ANDREAS SOFRONIOU   ISBN: 978-1-4467-5653-9

BUSINESS INFORMATION SYSTEMS, CONCEPTS AND EXAMPLES ANDREAS SOFRONIOU ISBN: 978-1-4092-7338-7 & 0952795639

A GUIDE TO INFORMATION TECHNOLOGY ANDREAS SOFRONIOU ISBN: 978-1-4092-7608-1 & 0952795647

CHANGE MANAGEMENT ANDREAS SOFRONIOU   ISBN: 978-1-4457-6114-5

CHANGE MANAGEMENT IN I.T.   ANDREAS SOFRONIOU ISBN: 978-1-4092-7712-5 & 0952725355

CHANGE MANAGEMENT IN SYSTEMS ANDREAS SOFRONIOU ISBN: 978-1-4457-1099-0

FRONT-END DESIGN AND DEVELOPMENT FOR SYSTEMS APPLICATIONS ANDREAS SOFRONIOU ISBN: 978-1-4092-7588-6 & 0952725347

I.T RISK MANAGEMENT ANDREAS SOFRONIOU   ISBN: 978-1-4092-7488-9   & 0952725320

THE SIMPLIFIED PROCEDURES FOR I.T. PROJECTS DEVELOPMENT ANDREAS SOFRONIOU ISBN: 978-1-4092-7562-6 & 0952725312

THE SIGMA METHODOLOGY FOR RISK MANAGEMENT IN SYSTEMS DEVELOPMENT ANDREAS SOFRONIOU ISBN: 978-1-4092-7690-6 & 095279568X

TRADING ON THE INTERNET IN THE YEAR 2000 AND BEYOND ANDREAS SOFRONIOU ISBN: 978-1-4092- 7577 & 0952795671

STRUCTURED SYSTEMS METHODOLOGY ANDREAS SOFRONIOU ISBN: 978-1-4477-6610-0

SYSTEMS MANAGEMENT   ISBN: 978-1-4710-4907-1   ANDREAS SOFRONIOU 978-1-4710-4891-3 & 978-1-4710-4903-3

INFORMATION TECHNOLOGY LOGICAL ANALYSIS ANDREAS SOFRONIOU ISBN: 978-1-4717-1688-1

MANAGEMENT OF I.T. CHANGES, RISKS, WORKSHOPS, EPISTEMOLOGY ANDREAS SOFRONIOU ISBN: 978-1-84753-147-6

THE MANAGEMENT OF COMMERCIAL COMPUTING ANDREAS SOFRONIOU ISBN: 978-1-4092-7550-3 & 0952795604

PROGRAMME MANAGEMENT WORKSHOP ANDREAS SOFRONIOU ISBN: 978-1-4092-7583-1 & 0952725371

THE PHILOSOPHICAL CONCEPTS OF MANAGEMENT THROUGH THE AGES ANDREAS SOFRONIOU ISBN: 978-1-4092- 7554-1 & 0952725363

THE MANAGEMENT OF PROJECTS, SYSTEMS, INTERNET, AND RISKS ANDREAS SOFRONIOU ISBN: 978-1-4092- 7464-3 & 0952795698

SYSTEMS ENGINEERING ANDREAS SOFRONIOU ISBN: 978-1-4477-7553-9

www.ingramcontent.com/pod-product-compliance
Lightning Source LLC
Chambersburg PA
CBHW061032050326
40689CB00012B/2781